Poker For Profit

The Ultimate Guide to Poker Theory and Strategy and How to Make Money From Poker

By

JAMES **K**ING

CONTENTS

INTRODUCTION

I want to thank you and congratulate you for purchasing the book Poker for Profit

This book contains proven steps and strategies on how to create an income from playing poker, and the techniques used to do this.

Perhaps you are great online but can't face a casino situation, perhaps you feel like you never get good enough cards to win or perhaps you feel you constantly get outdrawn. These things, although annoying should not take you out of the game! In this book we will teach you tips to enhance your game and build up enough chips to see you through those bad beats.

Whether you are totally new to Poker or have been playing for some time, this book has something for everyone.

.

1

TEXAS HOLD'EM. WHY THE APPEAL.

Despite what you may believe, Texas Hold'em is a very easy game to understand. The basics can be mastered in less than an hour if you look at it with a logical approach.

Every payer at the table is dealt two cards, face down. These cards are for you only and are called the hole cards. It goes without saying that every player will have a different two hold cards.

Next, five cards are dealt, in the middle of the table, all face up. These are called the community cards. Every payer at the table uses these five cards, together with their own two hole cards, to make the best hand using the best five cards as possible.

In between each round of dealing the cards there are four rounds of betting. The current or possible strength of your hand dictates your action in each of these betting rounds.

Pre-Flop.

Before any cards are dealt, two players must place, or post, a bet. This is a blind bet because nobody has received any cards yet and as such are called 'The Blinds'. The player immediately to the left of the dealer (or dealer button) must post a small bet, called the 'small blind' and the player immediately to the left of the small blind must post a larger bet, usually double the small blind, called the 'big blind'. The blind bets make sure that betting action always takes place before any of the community cards are dealt. The size of the blinds are dictated by the staking levels of the table. A table with stakes of $0.05/$0.10 means that the small blind is $0.05 and the big blind is $0.10

As the position of the dealer, or the dealer button, moves round the table in a clockwise direction, each player takes a turn of being in 'the blinds'.

Once the blinds have been placed, each player is dealt two cards, face down. Each player can look at their own cards but cannot see the cards of any other player, not show their own cards to anyone else. These cards are called your hole cards.

Now for the first round of betting.

How strong are your two hole cards. Are they worth investing money into the hand or should they just be folded (thrown away). At this point in time, you are basing the strength of your hand, or your possible final hand, on just two cards. Only you can see these two cards. Experience will tell you which hole cards are valuable and which are of little use.

Choices in a betting round.

During each betting round you have five basic choices.

Fold – If your cards do not seem to be strong and you do not wish to continue putting cash into the hand then you can fold, or throw away your cards by returning them, face down, to the dealer and take no further part in this hand.

Call – If someone has acted before you and has made a bet (or has placed a blind in the case of the pre-flop betting round) you can call the bet. This is done by paying the value of the bet into the pot. If the Big blind, or the initial bet, was 20 then you must pay 20 to call and continue in the hand.

Check – In later betting rounds, when no blinds have been placed, and no player has placed a bet before you, you can check. This means that you do not place any bet but still remain in the hand. The action then moves to the next player on your left.

Bet – If no player has placed a bet before it is your turn to act, then you can place a bet. The bet must be at least equal to the big blind, or all of your chips if the big blind is more than your remaining chip stack. To do this, simply declare the bet size and place your chips towards the middle of the table. Players after you must decide if they want to call your bet or fold their cards, depending on how strong they feel their hand is. If you bet all of your chips, going all in, you cannot bet any more in the hand but also cannot be made to fold your cards until the end of the hand. You are automatically in the hand until the very end where the best hand will win the pot at showdown.

Raise – If a player acting before you has already placed a bet, or the blinds have been played, you can make a raise. Your raise must be at least double current bet, or all of your chips if your chip stack is smaller than this. This makes the hand more expensive for following players to continue with. The other players, if they think their cards are not worth the extra cost, can fold.

Betting action.

The order of betting is always the same. The betting action always goes round the table clockwise starting with the player immediately to the left of the dealer. In the pre flop round of betting, the first player posts the small blind, the second player posts the big blind and the third player is the first to act. Once everyone has acted, by either folding their hole cards or matching the bets made, the bets are gathered into the centre of the table, 'the pot' and the next round of cards are dealt.

Community Cards.

After the first found of betting, pre plop, the community cards are dealt.

The Flop.

This is where the first three of the community cards are dealt, face up, onto the middle of the table. These cards are common to all players remaining in the hand. Every player can use these cards, along with their own two hole cards, to make the best five-card hand possible.

Now the second round of betting takes place. During this round, starting with the player immediately to the left of the dealer, you can choose to either check, call, raise or fold in the same way as you did with the pre flop betting. The difference now though is that you are basing your decision on not only your hole cards but the flop cards too.

Once all of the betting has finished the bets are once again gathered into the pot and the dealing continues.

The Turn.

The fourth community card is then dealt, face up, along side of the three flop cards.

All players still in the hand have another round of betting, with the same format as before and all bets collected into the pot before the dealing continues.

The River.

The fifth and final community card is then dealt alongside the other four community cards. This is the final card to be dealt and each player must now decide on the best hand they can make using any five cards from their available seven (community cards and hole cards).

Another round of betting happens and all remaining players at the end of the betting show their cards. This is the 'showdown' and the best five card hand on show wins the pot. If only one player remains at any point in the hand then they have won the pot and there is no need to show your cards to the dealer or the other players.

Showdown winner.

A poker hand is always made up of five cards, exactly five cards. At showdown, the best hand wins the pot. You do not need to use both of your hole cards to make your hand, indeed you do not need to use either of them. You just have to make the best five carded hand possible from the available cards. It doesn't matter which cards you use, as long as you use five of them.

There are lots of possible combinations of cards that can make a hand in poker. For example, three sevens and two tens make a 'full house', or five diamonds make a 'flush'. Each hand fits into a well established ranking order for determining the strength of the hand.

2

POKER HANDS

Royal Flush – The strongest possible hand in poker is the Royal Flush. This hand is made up of Ace, King, Queen, Jack and Ten, all the same suit.

Straight Flush – The second strongest hand is a straight flush. Five consecutive cards, all of the same suit.For example, two, three, four, five and six of hearts. If two players both have straight flushes, then the player with the highest cards win.

Four of a Kind – The next ranking hand is four of a kind. Four cards all of the same value, for example, four eights. If the four same value cards are all in the community cards, the player with the highest fifth card (the kicker) wins as every hand is always made up of exactly five cards.

Full house – A full house is five cards made up of three matching cards of one value and two matching cards of another. If more than one player has a full house, the highest three of a kind wins. If they have the same three of a kind then the highest pair wins.

Flush – Five cards, not consecutive, all of the same suit. If more than one player has a flush then the player with the highest card wins. If they both have the same high card, then the second highest card wins etc.

Straight – Five consecutive cards, of different suits. If more than one player has a straight then the highest card wins.

Three of a Kind – Three cards of the same value.For example, three fives. If more than one player has the same three of a kind then the highest other card, the kicker, or cards dictate the winner.

Two Pair – Obvious really, a pair is two matching value cards and two pair is two sets of two matching cards. If more than one player has two pair then the highest top pair wins. If they both have the same highest top pair then the highest second pair wins. If they both have the same two pair then the highest remaining fifth card, the kicker, wins.

Pair – Two cards of the same value. If more than one player has the same pair then the highest remaining card, the kicker, is the winner.

High Card – This is the weakest hand in poker and is based on the highest value card in your five card hand.

The higher up this list of ranking hands you find yourself, the stronger the strength of your hand. Hands at the bottom of the list, such as High Card, or a Pair, are seldom strong enough to win at showdown.

While you now know the basic rules of Texas Hold'em, and you know of the four rounds of betting and your basic options together with the ranking of each possible hand, it may seem a simple game. In reality, while it is very simple to learn the basics of the game, each hand can present very different situations and choices. It takes a lot of time and practice to master the game to a level that can be considered successful.

To help this there are a number of fundamental approaches and strategies that can help you develop your skills quicker.

3

BANKROLL MANAGEMENT

Taking care of your money.

You should always try to take care of your money, or you bankroll. This is the amount of cash that you can comfortably set aside for poker. Consider it an investment. It would be unwise to invest your money on a prospect with little or no chance of a profit. You should always try to minimise the losses at a poker table. Too many players are poor at bankroll management, playing at stakes which are too high, or playing weak starting hands hoping for the big payoff. These players and their bankroll are usually soon to be parted.

You should always try to find a reasonable balance between your need for making as much profit as possible and the need to minimise the step back you will take if you have a losing day at the tables. Ideally you want to win lots at each session while not losing too much if it doesn't go your way. This is called bankroll management.

There are a few simple guidelines to successful bankroll management. While you might feel that you want to push on and play for higher stakes to make more profits quicker, this is usually not a successful approach.

1 – Always join a table with 100 big blinds. This is often called a full stack or a big stack. It allows you to ride out the ups and downs of your chip stack during the game. If the blinds on a table are $0.01/$0.02 then you should sit at the table with $2 (100 x $0.02).

2 – Only ever use 2% of your bankroll at any one table. This protects your bankroll and minimises large losses. If your bankroll is $200, you should be aiming to join a table with $4. This would mean sitting at a table with blinds of $0.02/$0.04.

3 – Once you have increased your bankroll you can move up to higher stakes table, always following guidelines one and two. As your bankroll increases, so do the stakes you can safely play at. Likewise, if your bankroll decreases then the table stakes should decrease accordingly.

4 – A successful strategy for bankroll management involves knowing when to leave a table. Once your chip stack has reached double of what you sat down with, there is nothing wrong with standing and leaving the table. This usually applies to online games as there are always many more tables to choose from. This is often difficult to do in a live situation in a casino with only a few tables available. This method of 'banking the profits' once again helps to protect your bankroll. An alternative way of looking at it gives you the impression that you are 'killing' the table and are in total control. This would seem to say that you should stay at the table and keep increasing your winnings. Remember that other players can join your table as soon as a seat becomes available and higher level players are often looking for less experienced players with large chip stacks to plunder. Play it

safe and protect your winnings.

If you do not follow these simple guidelines and join a table with stakes too high for your bankroll then you will find that you become an easy target for the higher level players waiting to relieve you of your hard earned cash. Without a good bankroll management strategy it is unlikely that you will make any long term profits. Even the best players in the world have bad days at the table so you can expect that to happen to you. Make sure that when it does, you don't lose all of your bankroll.

4

PROFITABLE APPROACHES AND STYLES.

By far, the most profitable style of playing Texas Hold'em is the tight aggressive style. This is based on three very simple principles.

1 – **Tight Play** . This means that you are very selective with which starting hands to play. The majority of the starting cards, or hole cards, that you will receive throughout the game are obviously very weak and easy to fold pre-flop (such as eight of hearts and two of clubs, 8H,2C). Some hands can appear to be strong but are not, such as Queen ten for example. A tight player recognises that these types of hands are weaker than they seem and will not commit chips to continue in the hand. Likewise, after the flop some seemingly good hands are much weaker than they appear. Too many players continue a hand with only a pair, only to lose chips at showdown. Tight players recognise weak hands and can happily let them go while waiting for stronger cards.

2 – **Aggressive Play**. Aggressive players never just call. If a hand is worth playing then it's usually worth raising. Too many players just call a bet to 'see if I hit a better hand'. This is not a profitable way of playing. Your profits are usually the result of other players making mistakes. The easiest way of increasing other players mistakes is to put them under

pressure with a raise. Raising also removes more players from a hand who would otherwise just limp along in the hope of hitting it big at showdown. This can happen often and while some consider it to be bad luck, profitable players realize this is due to bad play on their part by letting the limping player reach showdown cheaply.

3 – **Position, position, position.** Whenever your opposing players have to act before you then you have an advantage. You can observe their moves before you need to make a move for yourself. Its often more profitable to make moves when playing in position. If your opposing player gets to act after you then they have the advantage over you. Profitable players really do make the most out of playing positions.

It is hard to understate how important good bankroll management , and a tight-aggressive approach to playing style is to being a profitable player.
As you progress through to playing higher limits you will develop your own style of play which will be based on these two fundamental approaches.

5

MASTERING THE PRE FLOP GAME.

The most important aspect of successful and profitable poker is the ability to choose the right starting hands. If you play a hand with the correct cards you minimise the risk of not holding the best hand and also reduce the likelihood of being placed into a situation where a difficult decision needs to be made later in the hand.

Learning which hands to play, when and how to play them and how to make sure you make the best profit from them is vital in order to achieve any sort of success. This chapter tries to give an overview of a basic strategy which will set you on the right road and allow you to tweak and develop to suit your own style.

As mentioned earlier, position within the hand plays a very important part in your success and which cards you should play. Your playing position in the hand has a strong influence of the selection, or range, of hands that you will play pre flop. The sooner you are to act after the dealer, the earlier your position is. The later your position, the more dominating control you have over the hand. The earlier your position, the stronger your hole cards need to be in order to be successfully played.

For most of this guide we will assume that you are playing on a ten handed table.

The positions at a table are divided into four roughly equal groups. Moving clockwise from the dealer you have the 2 blind positions. These are the weakest positions to be in. The next three positions can be thought of as being early positions. The next three are middle positions and the last two players to act are the late position. The dealer, in the strongest position, is often called the 'button' while the player to the right of the dealer is often called the 'cut off'.

If there are less than ten players at the table, then the earlier positions are dropped. For example, with nine players there is only one early position, with eight players there are no early positions. Seven players mean no early positions and only two middle positions.

In order to develop a sound approach to pre flop play, and maximise profits by avoiding playing cards that are too weak the following section gives you a set of guidelines to follow. You can choose to follow the guideline vigorously which will offer you the best protection against losses and the maximum profits, or you can choose to be more flexible and move boundaries as you feel comfortable with. Be aware though, that moving boundaries with either tighten or loosen your game play and could have an impact on your profits.

Starting 'hole' cards.

High Pairs. – These are Aces, Kings and Queens. These hole cards are premium hands and should be played as such. No matter which position you are in and no matter what action has been made before you, you should raise. Every time, without fail, raise. If you are worried about raising such premium hands then you really should not be sitting at the table. With good bankroll management you have already minimised the chance of large losses so that worry should not play a part in your thinking.

Middle Pairs. – These are Jacks, Tens and Nines. Regardless of your position you should always raise with these hold cards unless someone has already raised before you. In that case, a call will be the best move to continue through to the rest of the hand.

Low Pairs. – These are the remaining pairs. Eights down to Twos. These cards, while looking good, are not as strong as they appear. If a player acts before you and raises you should only call if in the late position otherwise a fold is usually the best move. If nobody has raised before it is your turn to act it is ok to call in the middle positions. These pairs should usually be folded from the early positions and the blinds. This might seem strange but remember, we are trying to play a tight-aggressive game and these cards are more often than not too weak by the time we reach showdown. Lots of hands, thus chips, and thus profits are lost by playing these low pairs.

Premium Ace. – Ace King or Ace Queen. Whether the same suit or different suits, these are premium hole cards and should be played the same way as high pairs. Raise every time.

Middle Aces. – An Ace with either a Jack or Ten or Nine. These can be very profitable cards if played correctly. If someone acting before you raises, then the easy and most profitable move is to fold. If you are in an early position, once again, these cards are not as strong as they appear and as such should be folded. If a player before you acts and simple calls, then the optimum move is to play a simple call. If all players before you have acted and have folded, you can simply call when in middle position or raise when in the late position. Remember, position is important. A raise in late position with all other players folding before you will often win the hand without needing to see a flop.

Low Suited Aces. – An Ace with any other card of the same suit. Fold to any raise with these weaker cards. Call in late position if any other player has called before you. Raise in late potion if all other players acting before you have folded. Once again, a high chance of winning the pot without seeing a flop.

Face Cards.– Either a King, Queen or Jack. Both cards the same suit or different. If any player before you raises, then fold. Regardless of position. These cards should again be folded in early or middle positions. If you are in late position and all players have folded before you, then a raise once again is the best option. If any players have called before you, then simply call to see the flop cards.

Suited Connectors. – These are two connecting cards, eight nine for example, or five six, that are of the same suit. Not always a profitable hand to play but they do have possibilities. These should be played exactly the same way as two face cards. Fold to any raise, call in late position with any other player calling before you or raise in late position if all players have folded before you.

All other starting cards should be folded. Remember, a dollar saved is a dollar not lost.

As you progress though the poker tables you will often find players playing strange hands, such as Ten Seven, saying that they are their favourite cards. This is usually due to once or twice when they played them they hit lucky and scored big. Players always seem to remember the big winning hands while not remembering the many times they played these cards and lost valuable chips. This is human nature but don't be fooled into thinking like that. It's not a good idea to have 'favourite' hands when playing poker for profit.

Mastering the Raise.

There is a distinct skill in raising the correct amount. Raising too much with Premium hole cards will often put other players on the back foot and they fold, losing you the chance of winning more chips. Raising too small often allows more players to stay in the hands with marginal hole cards with a chance of hitting lucky before the flop and 'bad beating' you for the pot. Changing the amount you raise can often be used by other players to indicate the strength of your hand. It is a good idea to stick to a strict set of rules when raising. This keeps the raise the same each time and does not give any helpful hints to the other players.

If no player before you raised, then a little counting tells you how much to raise. A good starting point is to raise three big blinds plus one big blind for every player who has called before you.

For example. If your table has blinds of 10/20 it means that the big blind has put 20 chips into the pot. If you are in the late position and two players before you have called then your raise, should it be required, is simple 3 + 2 big blinds, 5 big blinds which means you raise to 100. Using this simple calculation you hide the strength of your hand whilst raising sufficiently to stop mediocre hands from staying in and hitting lucky. It doesn't always work as some players will play their 'favourite' hand regardless but this approach minimises losses.

If someone before you has raised, then use a similar calculation three times the raise plus one raise for each player called.
For example, playing the same 10/20 table. If a player raises to 60, and one player calls before your turn to act, your raise would be 4 times the raise, ie 4 x 60 which gives a raise of 240.

Multiple raises before its your turn to act. If one player raises, and a second player re-raises before it is your turn to act then your solution is simple. Only the top premium starting hands are worth playing in this situation. Unless you have Ace Ace, King King or Queen Queen then you fold. Getting involved in this hand would not be profitable. If you do have one of the top three starting hands, your move is simple. ALL IN.

Once you have a clear understanding of the starting hands that you should be playing you will be better prepared to play profitable poker. Selecting the correct starting hands is a main skill that is vital for success. Too many players lose profits by playing too many weaker hands that they think are strong. By selection the correct starting hands you can help avoid difficult situations after the flop cards have been dealt by avoiding marginal decisions. Be aware though, especially at lower limit tables, many players will call regardless of their starting hands. By correct card selection you can maximise your profits from these players. Remember, you can't lose chips if you are not in the hand. A chip saved is as good as a chip won in most cases.

6

PLAYING AFTER THE FLOP

Assuming that your starting cards were sufficient to keep you in the hand to see the flop we now get to the core of Texas Hold'em. What to do after the flop.

Now is not the time to sit back and hope for the best. Now is the time to put your aggressive approach into play, but always with caution. You should have played very close attention to all of the play before the flop, how did the other plays bet, how did they act. These little signs, even with online poker, can often tell a lot about where you are within the hand. Larger than usual raises, very quick calls, long slow thinking times, all of these 'tells' can give you an advantage. That's why we always try to be the same, trying not to show the strength, or weakness, of our hands.A lot of the way you now play your hand will depend on mathematics. Don't be too worried, it isn't rocket science level thinking, but it is important. We will go into the mathematics a little later but for now we will look at the basics.

How did the Flop develop your hand.

Made hands.

A made hand can be considered as a hand that has been

completed, and could already be the winning hand. You now have five cards to work with (two hole cards and three community cards) and it is very possible that you have already completed a finished hand.

Of course, some of your made hands are stronger than others. Strong, made hands (often called Monster Hands) are Royal Flush, Straight Flush, four of a kind, full house , flush and a straight. Generally, the higher up the hand ranking your hand appears, the stronger your hand is. Obviously other players could also have a Monster Hand, so care should always be taken to consider that possibility. Always consider your hand carefully against what other hands are possible.

Example.

Your Hole cards are Jack Jack. The flop cards are Ten, Jack, Queen. Your made hand is Three of a kind, Jacks. But due to the flop cards, other possible made hands could be better than yours. Three Queens or a straight are possible. And this does not take into account the suits of the cards and possible flushes. While your hand is strong, and should be played as such, you should pay close attention to how other players respond to your play and act accordingly. If you raise with your three jacks and a following player re-raises, it is unlikely that your three jacks are the strongest hand and a fold is in order. Remember, a dollar saved is almost as good as a dollar won.

Other 'made' hands are not always as strong. Two pair can be very deceiving. Two pairs can only be thought of as a monster hand if both of your cards have paired with the cards in the flop. If you are holding a pocket pair and there is a pair on the flop, then your two pair is not a strong hand at all and more care should be taken.

Of all of the other possible 'made' hands, only two are worth continuing with.

Top Pair. If one of your hole cards has paired up with the highest community card then you have top pair. Not a Monster Hand but still a respectably strong hand.

Over Pair. If you are holding a pocket pair and all three community cards are lower than your pair then you have an over pair. Again not a Monster but still pretty strong if played right. Often this hand is better than top pair.

Draw Hands.

Draw hands are hands that are not yet complete but are very close, needing only one further card to make your 'made' hand. The strength of your 'draw' hand depends on how many cards are still available that could help your hand.
If you have four hearts, i.e., a flush draw. There are nine further hearts in the pack that could complete your flush. If you have a pair, i.e., two jacks, then there are only a further two cards in the pack that can complete your three of a kind. The flush draw is therefore stronger than the three of a kind draw.

Straight Draws.

If, between your starting hand and the community cards you have four connecting cards, six, seven, eight and nine for example, you have an Open Ended Straight Draw. It means that you are missing one more card, on either end of your sequence, to make a straight. Hence the Open Ended. There are 8 cards left in the pack which could complete your straight.

Monster Draw Hands.

Hands which combine both a straight draw and a flush draw are very strong hands indeed. This gives you a total of fifteen cards available to make your hand (the nine cards of the same suit and the three remaining high end straight cards, and the three remaining low end straight cards).

Gutshot Draw Hands.

These hands are not as strong as simple draw hands and only apply to straight draws. Where an open ended straight draw has a card at either end to complete the straight, the gutshot has a card missing from within the middle of the straight. For example, five, six, eight and nine means that you need the seven to complete the straight. This gives you only four cards available to improve your hand.

Double Gutshot.

If you are in the position, by using both of your hole cards and the three community cards, to have two possible gutshot draws, this is a double gutshot and is stronger. For example.Four, six, seven, eight, ten means that either a five or a nine can complete the straight, double gutshot, with eight available cards for improvement.

Over Cards.

If you have not already got a completed, made, hand nor do you have a draw hand then the only remaining hand of any note is overcards. If both of your hole cards are higher than the highest card on the flop you have overcards. Not a very strong hand but if you hit one of the following community cards to make a pair you will have top pair.

Betting after the flop.

As we have decided on a tight aggressive style to our play, and have reached the position of assessing our hand after the flop we need to make a decision on betting. In Texas Hold'em, it is often the aggressive player who has considered his play carefully that wins. With this in mind, every move made now must have a reason and a considered purpose.

7

BETTING

Reasons to bet.

Value.

Betting for value is the most basic form of betting. If you have a really strong hand you will want to get as much money into the pot as possible. Bigger pots mean more profits. Ideally you will want other players who have weaker hands to call and continue in the hand. This is betting for value. You must be careful though. Even though you think your hand is the strongest you must try to consider the hands of the other players. Which hands will call, which will fold, which will continue with a draw. You should try to keep your betting for value to times that you know your opponent is calling with a weaker hand.

Bluffing.

Another reason for betting is to bluff. This is a way of forcing the other players out of the hand so that you can win the pot. Bluffing is an art form in itself and should be considered carefully. Try to follow the bluffing guidelines.
Never bluff against more than one opponent.
Only bluff against players that you are sure will fold their

hand.

Only bluff when it is still possible that your hand can be improved with the following community cards.

Only bluff to represent a strong hand when the strong hand is obvious and it likely that your opponent has a weak hand

Example.

A good spot to bluff.

You raised pre flop with Queen Queen.

The flop cards are Ace Eight Six.

If you are in a late position and your opponent checks before you from an early position it is an ideal situation for the bluff. If your opponent has checked it is unlikely they have an Ace. If you make a bluff bet here and your opponent calls then you are still in decent shape. Another Queen gives you three of a kind and the other flop cards do not help any straight draws. Unless one of the other players are holding one of the three remaining Aces then its likely that they will fold and you win the pot. A classic example of a Bluff.

A poor Spot to Bluff.

You are holding the same Queen Queenhold cards, hearts and spades. The flop is six seven eight, all clubs. This flop does not lend itself to bluffing. There are far too many draw hands that are avaibable, as well as ready made hands. Flush draws and straight draws may not be prepared to bet from an early position but would be more than happy calling a bet that you might make. This is a classic No-Bluff situation.

Continuation Bets.

If you raised pre flop, and other players called then you have given an aggressive image. You have said, by your raise, that your hand is strong. Often this calls for a bet after the flop to continue representing a strong hand. A bet of this kind, a continuation bet, follows the similar reasoning as a bluff bet but you often have a much stronger hand. Be careful of making a continuation bet with a range of draw hands being available, unless you are confident that your hand will still be strong at showdown.

Protection.

Betting for protection is a much more common type of bet. Not every hand that you make is a Monster Hand. Most made hands will be strong enough but not Monsters. You may find that your hand is made but is vulnerable to players with Draw hands. Betting for protection is exactly that. You make a bet knowing that you have a made hand but not a strong made hand. Your opponent has now been put under pressure. Is it worth the extra chips to continue and try to complete their draw. Protection bets are strongly dictated by the maths and odds of the game, which will be covered later. Often enough you find that a fold follows your bet and you win the pot, thus protecting your weaker made hand.

Reasons not to bet

You will find that there are many reasons not to bet. Simply having no hand at all, or a weak hand, happens more times than you would care to remember. These are the times when you must wait, be patient. Do not commit more chips into a pot that you cannot win under normal circumstances. Simply fold to any bet and wait for the next hand to come along and hope for a better outlook.

Three very good, but deliberate, reasons not to bet can be introduced into your game strategy.

Slowplay.

If you play your hand in a way to make it appear to be weaker than it really is, then you are 'slowplaying' the hand. Instead of your usual aggressive approach to playing very strong hands, you make it appear that your hand is weak and hope to induce other players to bet or raise. Appearing weak encourages other players to over play weak hands or draws.

Example.If, after the flop, you have a straight flush.A Monster hand in anyone's world. If you played the hand aggressively, there would be very few hands that would call your bet. By appearing weak, and maybe checking, it almost forces players with weak hand, such as a pair or even a flush draw, to think that their hand is much stronger than it is. By not betting, your opponent commits chips to the pot, your pot. More profit.

Slowplay is usually a very poor way to play. Never slowplay against several opponents.Never slowplay on a flop that suits lots of draw hands.Never slowplay against passive opponents.Never slowplay a flush unless you are holding the Ace. Only slowplay when you are certain that the other player will over value their own hand and try to bet. You will find that with less experienced opponents, they will often be more willing to call a bet with a draw hand than bet after you check.

To induce a bluff.

This is very similar in format to slowplay. By making your hand appear weak, other players make try to make a bluff bet to win the pot there and then. More often than enough, the bet they make is bigger than you would expect. They are trying to bluff, and price you out of the hand.

Pot control.

Once the flop cards have been dealt you usually have a much better idea of the strength of your hand. If you have hit a monster, then you want to extract as much profit as possible from all of the players still in the hand. If you have only managed to hit a weak hand then ideally you do not want too many big bets so that any losses are minimal. This approach is called pot control.

Example. If, after the flop, you have a medium weak hand, maybe top pair. If the flop cards are not draw heavy, then your pair, which usually is not a very strong hand, maybe still be in control. If you were to make a bet, you are increasing the pot size with a weak hand. Subsequent community cards may make the board even more draw heavy and your hand will then not be strong enough. By betting you have wasted chips. By not betting, you are keeping the pot size small, and thus you are minimising your losses should that happen.

Total approach.

When making your decisions after the flop you need to be able to find a comfortable balance between your need to get the best value from strong hands, your need to keep the price low for your weak hands and the need to protect vulnerable hands by making the other players pay heavily to see the next community card.

The stronger your hand, the more you should try to play for value, the weaker your hand the more you should play for pot control.

How to play made hands.

This is probably the easiest option you may have. If you have a strong hand, then bet or raise. The more players that are still in the hand the stronger your hand needs to be. Only slowplay with very strong hands. The more draws that the flop cards produce, the more expensive you should make it for other players to remain in to see the next community cards. If you have a weak hand, then pot control should be your aim.

How to play draws.

To be able to play draw hands successfully you need to have a sound understanding of pot odds. This will be covered later in the book. Generally, you should be very passive about playing draws. Only play strong draw hands and never chase a medium or weak draw. You with generally be behind at showdown. You should only play a strong draw hand aggressively when you are sure that your opponent will fold. Never aggressively play a draw hand with several players still in the pot.

Overview.

You now have a basic understanding of how to play after the flop. Understanding the idea of pot control or betting for protection is a vital skill that all good poker players need to master. You never want to bet big with weak hands and always want to extract the maximum profit when holding a monster. Likewise, it is important that you do not let the other players see the remaining community cards too cheaply, letting them hit draw hands you wouldn't expect.

Always play tight, avoid less solid plays.
Always play aggressively with strong hands and take the lead rather than always letting other players bet for you to call.
Always remember to play in position.

Playing after the turn and the river are very similar and follow the same general guidelines.

8

POKERS MATHEMATICS.

Throughout the previous chapters we have touch on areas that need a little calculating in order to gain a better insight into the strength of your hand. This is usually for play after the flop. Play before the flop follows very strict and easy to follow guidelines.

We have already explained the strengths and weaknesses of your hole cards.

The interesting, and more complicated situation is after the flop cards have been dealt. Often in Texas Hold'em you still do not have a made hand after the flop. Often you have a draw hand. This could mean, that at that exact moment, before the turn and the river cards are dealt, your hand may be behind but the chances of improving to get the strongest hand might be high. You need only one card to complete your hand. This card is called the 'Out' card and quite often you have several draw cards available.

The number of out cards available gives you how realistic your chances are of making your draw hand.

Example.

Your hole cards are six and seven of clubs. The flop cards are five clubs, eight clubs and ace of hearts. You have a pretty strong draw hand. You have an opened ended straight draw, a flush draw and an open ended straight flush draw. In this case there are quite a few cards left to come that could make your hand. Any club would make your hand into a flush. There are 13 clubs in the pack and there are four on show to you. This leaves nine remaining clubs with which to complete your flush hand. Your open ended straight draw requires either a four or a nine. There are four fours in the pack and four nines, that gives you eight cards which could complete your straight. Two of these cards, the four of clubs and the nine of clubs would give you a straight flush but these cards have already been counted in the flush 'out' cards. Leaving six further cards that could complete your straight.

Overall there are fifteen cards which could complete your hand.

It's a simple enough idea to be able to count the number of out cards available for you but in practice, with the pressure of the table and the prospect of losing your hard earned cash, it becomes harder.

Hitting your out.

Once you have calculated the number of out cards that you have available, the next step is to work out the probability of this happening. This is called the 'odds'.

Try to follow this process.

In the example given above, you have fifteen out cards. There are 52 cards in the pack, but five of them are already known to you. This leaves 47 cards.

Divide the number of out cards by the number of available cards to get the probability of hitting one of your out cards on the turn (the next community card.

15 divided by 47 gives 0.319 or put a different way, 31.9% chance of hitting your card. In poker, odds are usually given as probabilities, In this case, 31.9% is 31.9 times out of every hundred, which is roughly one in every three times. This is given as '1 to 2' meaning that on average, there are two misses for every hit.

Some of the maths can be pretty complicated so there is no reason not to make things simple.
A simplified route for the example is as follows.

15 outs available
47 cards left, which is roughly 50.
15 from 50 is the same as 30 from 100.
30 from 100 is 30%, or almost 1 to 2.

Simple calculations but a very similar result. Just remember that the probability of hitting your out using the simplified method is slightly less than using the complete method but it is close enough to give you the information you need.

Once the turn card has been dealt then you need to do a similar calculation for the river card unless you have hit. The difference this time is there are only 46 cards remaining. Slightly different (increased) odd of hitting your out card.Using the simplified method though the result would be the same.Saves you working it all out again.

For the above example, you have roughly 30% chance of hitting one of your out cards on the turn, and 30% on the river. This gives 60% chance of hitting one of your out cards before showdown.

If, for this example, your opponent has hit the ace, and top pair, he may be ahead of your draw hand after the flop. But remember, you have 60% chance of hitting one of your outs which will make a hand better than top pair so you have the highest probability of winning the hand by showdown.

Some of the more common odds are given below.

- Flush Draw and Open Ended Straight Draw – 15 outs
- Flush Draw and Pair – 14 outs
- Open Ended Straight Draw and Pair – 13 outs
- Flush Draw and Gutshot – 12 outs
- Flush Draw – 9 outs
- Open Ended Straight Draw – 8 outs
- Two Pairs – 4 outs
- Gutshot – 4 outs
- Pocket pair to a set – 2 outs

Remember, to use the simple calculation of odds, simply double the number of outs with one card to come and double again with two cards to come.

Example.

Open Ended Straight Draw – 8 outs, 16% chance of hitting with one card to come (accurate calculation is 17%) and 32% chance of hitting with two cards to come (accurate calculation is 34.4%)

For most hands, the simple calculation is close enough. Both methods giving you pot odds of roughly 2 to 1

Pot Odds and Profits

Pot odds can be used to calculate the possible profits compared to the stake you need to commit to the pot. This is often seen as a risk/reward ratio. By doing a simple comparison of the pot odds (the odds that you will hit one of your out cards) to the pot odds (the amount you could win for your stake) you can get an indication of the profitability of your next play.

Example.

Let us continue with the same example, Hole cards six, seven clubs. Flop five clubs, eight clubs, ace hearts.
We have already determined that we will hit one of our out cards one time out of every three.
If, for this hand, the pot already contains $12 but to continue with your hand you need to call a bet of $3.
You are risking $3 into a pot with a reward of $12.
If this hand was to be played out, one time in every three you will win. The other two times you will lose.
Lets look at the profits. When you win, you risk $3 and win $12.
When you lose you risk $3 and win nothing.
This means that for every three times the hand is played, you are risking $9 and winning$12. For this reason it is worth playing this hand in the long run. This is because, over time, pot odds will give you a net profit.
For this example, we risk $3 to win $12. Our pot odds can be thought of as possible reward : risk required. For this

example the pot odds are 12:3 or 4:1
The pot odds ate 4:1 and your out odds are 2:1.

You should always continue with the hand of the pot odds are larger than your out odd because over the longer period of time you will see profit. If the pot odds are lower then over time you will lose.

Remember though, that this example only considers the odds of hitting the out card on the next community card. You may have two cards to come and this makes a difference to your decisions. Of course, with two cards to come there are two rounds of betting so the risks may be more costly. Some players like to consider the game all the way to the showdown, calculating two rounds of pot odds (sometimes called implied odds) based on what they think will happen after the next community card.

As our game is based on a tight-aggresive style, it is usually best just to consider one round of betting at a time.

.

9

TOURNAMENT POKER OVERVIEW.

So far we have dealt with the basic fundamental approaches towards successful and profitable poker. Everything should seem straightforward, if you decide on a strategy of which hands to play, and in what position, most of the initial decisions will be made for you. The more you play, the more you will develop your understanding and your approach will gradually change to suit the style that you are most comfortable with and with which you find the most success with. All of these approaches are aimed at cash games. A single poker table with up to nine other players and constantly changing and developing.

Your bank roll management should mean that if, on a cash table, you lose all of your chips you can reload instantly. It is not unusual for successful poker players to finds that they need to reload at times. The swings of fortune and 'bad beats' can cause everyone problems but over time they become less significant as long as a sensible approach is used.

Tournament poker strategy is very much different. All of the fundamentals are exactly the same. The approach towards each hand is very similar. Your 'fold or play' strategy could also be similar but the main difference, and it is a significant difference, is that once you lose all of your chips then that's it. Game over. Putting this aside, tournament poker is an ideal way of beginners and developing poker players to get lots of experience, play lots of hands, for a relative small amount of cash. The safety net is always present in tournament poker. Once you have paid your entry to the tournament then you cannot lose any more money. The losses are fixed at the entry fee. If you play well and make a good run, running deep into the tournament it is possible to make a serious addition to your poker bankroll.

There are some tournaments which allow you to rebuy a starting stack, and some tournaments allow you 'double chance' entry of two bites at the cherry for your entry, but by far the most common tournament is a single buy, knock out format.

When thinking about tournament formats and structures it is best to consider every tournament that you enter to be of this format. It is unwise to enter a rebuy tournament planning to make several rebuys. This may, of course, happen but it is much better to approach with the mind set of one entry cost and making sure that you play to win, not to lose all of your chips. It is a very negative approach to enter a tournament with the intention of spending more money on the rebuy. Often it means that the winnings you could get are not as appealing as they initially seem.

Example.

A local casino may be running a $5 rebuy tournament. The usual breakdown of prizes for the normal field of 50 runners could be as follows.

The usual buy in's could be (assuming an average of 2 rebuys per person)

1st – $280
2nd – $165
3rd - $115
4th - $85
5th - $60
6th - $45

This means that if you manage to finish in 6th Place, prize money of $45 for your single buy in of $5 is a much better return that for your entry plus two rebuys of $15.

Still a profit but much less of a return on your investment.

Likewise for double chance tournaments. (Here you get two lots of starting stacks for your entry fee.) You may get two lots of 10, chips on entry. You usually have the option of taking wither one lot of 10,000 at the start of the game and the second lot at any time you choose (usually when you lose lots of chips so are at a disadvantage on the table) or take both lots at the start of the game so that you have a chip advantage on the table.

The more common method is to start with one lot and keep the second lot in reserve. If you take both lots at the start you will find that there are always a couple of other player doing the same so that you do not really have that much of a chip advantage and as the rest of the players also have a single stack you are not disadvantaged. You have these chips in reserve and if you play tight and slowly build up your chip stack then the second lot of chips taken at the break are a welcome bonus.

For the purposes of developing a tournament strategy we will assume that the tournament is a single buy, no rebuy, no re-reentry tournament. Once you have lost your chips then that's it, game finished.

10

BASIC TOURNAMENT STRATEGY.

The most important strategy in tournament poker is the most simple. The main aim for most of the game is survival, protect your chips at all costs as once they are gone then the game is over for you.

You should have some sort of awareness of how many chips you have and how many chips the other players have.

Another important part of tournament play which differs completely from cash play is the blind structure. On a cash table the blinds remain fixed. You may sit at a cash table with $50 and the blinds could be $0.50/£1.00 and they will remain at that level for the complete time you are playing. In tournament play the blind structure is always changing. The blinds start small, usually very small compared to the starting stack of chips, but the blinds increase at regular levers. Blind levels of twenty to thirty minutes are quite normal. This means that every twenty minutes the blinds will increase.

A typical blind structure is given below.

1	25	50	+0:00
2	50	100	+0:20
3	75	150	+0:40
4	100	200	+1:00
5	125	250	+1:20
6	150	300	+1:40
7	200	400	+2:00
8	300	600	+2:20
9	400	800	+2:40
10	500	1000	+3:00
11	600	1200	+3:20
12	1000	2000	+3:40
13	1500	3000	+4:00
14	2000	4000	+4:20
15	3000	6000	+4:40
16	4000	8000	+5:00

Every twenty minutes the blinds increase. The starting level, Level 1, has blinds of 25/50 but after play has passed the two hour mark the blinds have increased to 200/400
The purpose of the blind increases it to ensure that the tournament progresses. As the blinds increase it forces player with low chip stacks to play rather than sit and fold every hand. This makes sure that the tournament reaches a conclusion within a reasonable time scale.

Example of effectiveness of blind increases.

The increasing blind structure makes a difference to the value of your chips. If, using the above blind structure for example, your starting stack of 5000 chips you are starting the tournament with 100 big blinds. This is often the best way to think of your chip value.

If you approach the tournament with a very tight strategy you may find that after 20 minutes you have been dealt twenty hands and have not played a single hand, folding each time. During the twenty hands you have been in the small blind position twice and the big blind position twice, costing you a total of 150 chips. Now, 150 compared to the total chip stack of 5000 may seem insignificant but if the value of your chips is considered it looks totally different.

After 20 minutes you now have 4875 chips and the blinds are now 50/100. You now have just over 48 Big blinds left in your chip stack.

Twenty minutes of extremely tight play has seen your effective chips stack reduced from 100 big blinds to 48 big blinds. A big difference.

If you follow the same logic for the next twenty minutes the difference becomes even more marked. In fact, not playing a hand for an hour means that you are left with an effective stack of just twenty big blinds.

Now, things are not always as bad as they seem. The same is happening for the other players on the table and this must be taken into account within your strategy for the tournament.

A very effective way to start a tournament is to keep your play very tight and very aggressive. This approach should be very familiar to you from the previous chapters in the book. In a usual tournament of about fifty players, the majority of the players will have a different approach. They will see their starting stack and being very large and so they can play in a much more open style. Far too often you will see players calling blinds or even small raises with a wider range of hands that you would expect. This is partly because of greed (I have lots of chips so I can afford to lose a few in the hope of hitting it lucky) and partly because of human nature (they feel they can afford to lose a few small pots without much problem.

Try to take a 'sit and wait' approach to these hands. If your strategy dictates that you will fold 9 10 off suite then do not be tempted to make a small call in the hope of hitting the right cards. In the long term this, as you are well aware, is not a profitable approach. By opening your range your chips will bleed away slowly and your effective stack will become less and less as the blinds increase. Make sure that you do not blow your chip stack too early in the game. Don't waste your chips on incorrect calls and wrongly timed moves. Tournament play is similar to cash in that way, don't waste chips. A chip saved is a chip earned. Start with your strategy, pick your spots from within your tight range and play aggressively. If things go to plan, you will usually find that you have increased your chips significantly after the first few blind levels. Usually at the expense of the more open, risk taking players. It is not unusual to find that almost half of the players have lost all of their chips by the end of the third blind level. Make sure that this doesn't happen to you by sticking to your tight aggressive approach.

The best approach for a beginner in a tournament is easy to follow. Play a very tight aggressive style at the start and through the first couple of levels and loosen up your play, opening the range of your starting hands as the tournament progresses. Try not to get caught up in big chip confrontational hands too early on unless you have a really big hand. There is no need at all to rush things at the early stages of a tournament and the risk losing too many chips in the beginning of the game is a big problem facing many beginners.

Playing with this tight strategy also gives you time and opportunity to observe the other players on your table and develop an understanding of the way they are playing, becoming aware of the range of their starting hands and how they play big hands. Information like this will help I the later stages of the tournament.

11

MIDWAY TOURNAMENT STRATEGY

If you have maintained your very tight but very aggressive approach then you should find that you are still in reasonable shape by the time the mid section of the tournament approaches. This is a wide range of the tournament. Most of the inexperienced players, or the loose wild player, and the chancers, will have been eliminated. You should still be in a situation where you can reasonably expect to have around twenty or thirty big blinds worth of chips. Now is the time to start to loosen up a little bit. As you get deeper into the tournament (last longer) then you must adapt your playing approach to suit the situation.

Example.

While in position of button you have been dealt AJ off suit. Early on in the tournament you may be tempted to fold this hand for several reasons.

1 – While a pretty reasonable starting hand it still leaves many starting hands stronger that could also be available and the aim at the start of the tournament is to protect chips at all costs.

2 – Early on there will be more inexperienced or looser players that may play with a weaker starting hand but hit a

lucky card.

3 – It is difficult to be aggressive with this hand while there may be several players at the table who might be willing to call as the chip cost seems low.

If there are five players acting before you then playing this type of hand usually leads to problems. Five players means ten cards available for people to hit a matching card so there is less chance of your AJ playing out to be the winning hand. It is probably best to fold this hand at this point in the tournament with so many callers acting before you.

Later in the tournament it changes though. The same hand in the same position would probably not have as many callers before it is your turn to act. Most players will consider the higher blind level as not worth the risk, and rightly so. This would probably mean that less people would call. You will also find that the players left at this stage should all be a little more experienced than the players already eliminated. If you have been playing a very tight game then these players would have noticed. If, in this situation, you were to raise a standard size raise, as discussed before, then unless they were holding a very big starting hand they would tend to fold for several reasons.

1 – Players with weak starting hands would have already folded, leaving you facing less people pre flop.

2 – If another player has a very big starting hand, say AA, KK, AK then at this stage in the tournament they would have raised before action has reached you. This gives you enough information to be able to fold at no cost in chips.

3 – Any player with a medium starting hand who might want to try his luck and call to hope to hit, will usually fold to a raise made after their call.

In this situation a raise has several benefits. Of course, you still have a minority of players (the small and big blinds) to act after you but it minimizes the risk of being re-raised. Especially if you have demonstrated a tight approach to the other players on the table.

By opening your range of starting hands and playing in a less tight manner you can take advantage of decent cards on good positions much more than you could do in the early stages of a tournament.

At the mid stages of a tournament you will find that more players are starting to open up their starting hand ranges and you should expect other players to take the same approach as you do. Your main focus should still be to prevent chip loss but start to collect chips at each opportunity as it arises. Tournament play is a long drawn out game and a tournament is never won by playing one massive hand aggressively. The chip leader at the first break (usually after three of four levels) is rarely the chip leader at the second break and almost never wins the tournament. Long, selective, controlled and correct play will see a slow gradual increase to your chip stack.

12

THE BUBBLE

This stage in the tournament is often the most excitable and enjoyable. But it can also be the most hazardous and stressful stage for players with relatively low stacks. The bubble is the point in the tournament where the next two or three players who are eliminated will win nothing but the remaining players will be in the cash. A tournament of 55 players will usually pay prize money to the last six players, When the number of remaining players reaches seven or eight it can be thought of as 'the bubble'. You are now at a position of being only a few places away from being profitable for the tournament.

Imagine the situation of playing for four or five hours, to reach the bubble stage, and get eliminated just one place away from the money. This same thought is going through the mind of pretty much every other player left in the tournament. It is important that you remain in control during this stage. If you have a relatively small stack when you reach this point (for example 16000 chips, you might have more than your starting stack of 5000 but if effect, with blinds of 500/1000 you only have 13 big blinds worth left) you should adopt a more conservative approach. Tighten back up, take no risks, Approach every single hand with extreme caution. Be aware that even a small slip up at this stage will cost you a significant portion of your remaining chip stack. Concentrate on survival, fold every hand that is not an absolute monster hand. At this point you should only really be playing premium hands such as AA or KK. Any other hand should be folded. The aim is to survive.

One tip for this approach is to use reverse psychology. Earlier in the game you should have been looking at your starting hands, looking at the number of cards available for your improvement, looking at the lay of the other players on the table, and looking for the correct reason to be positive and play the hand. At this point you should be looking for reasons NOT to play your hand. Look for reasons to fold. You may find that on occasions you have folded the winning hand but in the long term it will work out more profitable. Folding a hand will cost you no chips. Calling a hand will cost you at least one big blind worth of chips, a large percentage of your remaining stack.

The reverse is the case for players with very large chip stacks. If you have managed to reach the bubble stage and have a large healthy chip stack, say eighty or ninety big blinds worth, then now is the time to apply the pressure. You should be looking for every opportunity to put pressure on the players with smaller stacks. These players are all looking at the bubble point and are usually trying to survive long enough to make the cash positions. Remember, no player really wants to play for five hours and lose out a cash payment at the very last minute by playing a loose and weak hand. As a player with a large chip stack you can now open your range and play hands that earlier in the tournament would have been folded instantly. Take every chance available to put a small stack player all in. (making a raise that is bigger than their complete stack). Most players will automatically fold to such a raise unless they are holding premium starting cards. It is important to consider your position with this style of player.

Example.

You are on the button position and have 78 BB chips. A player in mid position with 11BB has simply called the blinds. All other players acting before you have folded. Your starting cards are JT off suit. You can gain several pieces of information from this play.

1 – You are more than likely only going to be playing your starting hand against one player. If you raise then the small and big blind, unless they are holding a monster premium hand ,will fold to your raise, trying to avoid losing chips in the bubble stage.

2 – It is unlikely that your opponent has a premium hand. By simply calling the blind they are usually hoping for a cheap way to see the flop cars and hope to hit on the flop, thus giving them a big enough hand to risk all of their chips with.

3 – If your opponent does indeed have a premium hand such as AA or KK then the usual method of play would be to raise, usually all in, and collect the blinds when everyone else folds. If they did get a caller then they had a high chance of doubling their chip stack.

In this situation is usually a good play to raise the other player. Raising enough to mean that the player is all in, say 15BB gives them a simple choice to make. They either call with all of their chips and risk their tournament being non profitable or they fold and wait for a premium hand or to wait till other players have been eliminated and the bubble situation is no longer in play. Usually they will fold and it is easy chips for you, you will have taken their call and the blinds. Free chips almost. If the other player does indeed call then it is more than likely that they have a better starting hand than you and you are at a disadvantage. There is always the chance that you out draw your opponent and id your starting hand is a medium strength on then you are usually not less than a 25% underdog at minimum. Even if you lose the hand you have lost ten or so BB's and are still left with a commanding chip stack of almost seventy BB's. Not a bad position to be in.

Some things to note on this approach.

1 – Only put pressure on short stacked opponents, never call an all in with medium strength starting cards in the hope of out drawing them. It is reckless to risk chips, even a relative small amount, on hoping to out draw an opponent. If they have starting cards that are strong enough to commit their complete stack to and risk being eliminated from the tournament at this late stage then they will usually be in a much stronger starting position than you. The best approach is to fold and save your chips; maybe another player will call the all in raise which could have the same effect of elimination a player. In this position, using the pot odds to justify a call is not the correct approach.

2 – Be aware of the other player on the table with large chip stacks. Especially the players who are behind you and still to act. You really only want to apply the pressure on players who have relatively small stacks, not become involved in a hand with another large stacked player with less than premium starting cards.

Example.

If we use the previous example. You are on the button position and have 78 BB chips. A player in mid position with 11BB has simply called the blinds. All other players acting before you have folded. Your starting cards are JT off suit.

You attempt to put pressure on the weaker stacked player by raising to 15BB and the player in the BB position decides to re-raise you to 30BB then it is an instant fold. Your starting cards are sufficient to apply pressure to a small stacked player but are not good enough to mix it up with another equally large stacked player who has starting cards strong enough to re-raise you. The same pressure has been applied to the small stacked player and you should simply fold and wait for a new position.

A point to note on raising against short stacked players. If you raise enough to make it an all in bet for the player, say 14 BB raise when they are holding 11BB then you are giving them a simple choice. It's either all in or fold. A coin flip of a choice, with two alternatives. If you apply a more selective pressure and raise so that if they were to call then they would use more than half of their stack. Say, raising 7 BB when they are holding 10BB then it applies more pressure. It is now not a simple call or fold situation for all or nothing. In effect they are really not in a position to simply call as it would leave them with an extremely low chip stack which effectively finishes their tournament. They now have a greater dilemma. Human instinct makes them think more about the options. They can fold, success to you; they can call, you are risking less chips to see the flop, success to you; or they can then re-raise all in. Most players will find this option a little more stressful. It is very difficult to re-raise all in without premium cards. They will, at the back of their minds, have the thought that they can call and still have some chips left with which to play past the bubble and into the cash positions. Logically they should simply fold or re-raise all in, but the added option and extra thought needed to make a decision often applies more pressure and as a result the player tends to fold more often. Over time, this measured raise will be more profitable for your play during the bubble stages.

Playing short handed

As you survive deeper into a tournament you will, at times, find that you are playing on short handed tables. If there are 21 players remaining then you will be in a situation of 3 tables with 7 players each. If you have reached the last 12 players then you will find that you are playing on 2 tables of 6 players each. Shorthanded play is an important part of the tournament strategy.

During shorthanded play you should try to adopt a more aggressive approach. Your medium starting cards become more valuable and stronger. Entering a pot with six players holding starting cards of JQs puts you in a stronger position than entering a pot of ten players with the same starting cards. Your range should open up and you should play less tight. The aggressive approach should not really change though. The only real difference is that the value of your medium range starting hands increases. You may often find yourself in a situation where you are involved in a hand with weaker cards than you would have normally played. This is understandable. You take so much time and effort into developing your tight aggressive approach that it feels unnatural to play such hands. This is expected. You need to be adaptable in tournament play and this is one such change you should adapt to.

Mathematically it is justified. If you are playing a ten handed table, every three rounds, thirty hands, you will be the Big Blind three times and the Small Blind three times. This means that for every thirty hands you are committing 4 ½ BB worth of chips. If you were to adopt a very tight strategy you might find that you have folded every hand in these thirty. Not too much of a problem in the early stages with full tables.

If, however, you are playing on a six handed table in the later stages of a tournament, for the same thirty hands you will have faced the Big Blind five times and the Small Blind five times. That is 7 ½ BB of chips lost. Quite a significant difference, especially when your chip stack may be down to less than twenty BB's. You will find that by adopting your super tight approach will mean that your chip stack will slowly 'leak away' as you are constantly paying the blinds. For this reason and this reason alone you should loosen up your starting range and play more hands. Playing super tight on short handed tables quickly reduces your chip stack and sometimes even eliminates you from the tournament.

13

FINAL TABLE

So, you have started the tournament with a tight aggressive approach. You have survived the reckless play of others during the first few levels and passed though the bubble stage. You have reached the final table.

If you have managed to get this far with a relatively small chip stack then the approach that you used o get through the bubble stage should remain in place. Approach every hand with care, fold most hands that are not premium hands and play your premium starting cards, if you should be lucky enough to receive them, aggressively. The blinds are usually large by the time the final table has been reached to it is difficult to progress further unless you have a significant chip stack. Pick your spot, choose your starting cards wisely and play aggressively. With a relative small chip stack it is often enough to play aggressively and raise big and take the chips from the players in the blind positions when everyone folds. This means that, by winning the value of a small and big blind, you have assured another round of play of nine or ten hands which gives you a little more time to find the premium hand and double your chip stack.

If you have managed to get this far with a massive chip stack then once again you should approach the table play in the same way that you did during the bubble level. Apply pressure on the players with weak stacks and avoid mixing it up with players of large chip stacks unless you have a massive premium hand. The players with the small stacks will soon be eliminated as the blind structure takes its toll on their relatively small chip stack. Take the most you can from this opportunity and steal chips where suitable from the players with the smaller stacks. There is no real need for you to open up your range of hands for calling raises. Remember; let the blind structure eliminate the two or three smaller stacked players.

If you have reached the final table with a significantly large chip stack that put you in an obviously chip leader position then you should take the opportunity to apply pressure on all of the other players on the table. The players with smaller stacks will be hesitant in playing without premium hands as their tournament survival is on the line so you can 'bully' them and slowly increase your chip stack. The players with medium sized chip stacks will not want to risk their tournament position by risking less than perfect starting hands against a player with such a massive chip advantage. The other players with larger chip stacks will also not want to risk their tournament position by gambling against a large chip stack unless they have premium hands. This is an ideal time for you to apply pressure, and stress, to the other players with well thought out and structured raises. Try to be aware of not only your own chip stack sixe, but also the size of the stacks of the other players. Careful consideration of the position from which you are playing should also be made. Pick each spot carefully and maximize the returns from every hand you play.

Remember than in normal tournament pay out structures, the prize money rises slowly between the lower winning positions and rises sharply between the final few positions. Surviving to allow another player to be eliminated before you provides a bigger pay out the deeper in the tournament that you get. This is often on all players' minds and you can take advantage of this by applying pressure. Very few players, with relative small stacks, will be willing to risk elimination in third place with average starting cards and win $120 when they could fold, survive and maybe 'ladder up' to second place and win $180 when the two big stacks tangle and one is eliminated.

Heads up

So, you have found yourself in a great position. You have reached the final two players. Play at this stage of the tournament is very different to play in other stages. If possible, you should try and practice heads-up play so that you are ready. In this situation you are facing just one other starting hand. This means that your starting cards go up in value significantly. Starting hands that you would have instantly folded in other stages of play suddenly become very playable. A starting hand such as A6 off suit would have been totally unplayable pre flop in any other situation of the tournament but in head-up those starting cards are massive.

Starting hands such as these are always suitable to be played as premiums. The value of an ace in heads up is Massive and should always be played as such. This type of hand should always produce a raise. This wider range of starting hands that you can raise with will apply lots of extra pressure on your opponent. If you do not open up your range like this then your chip stack will be reduced to nothing in almost no time. Remember, that with only two players you are always paying a blind, either the big blind or the small blind.

Your opponent will also try to apply pressure in the same way. Often the heads up situation does not last very long. Each player soon finds a starting hand that they think is strong enough to play, a raise, a re-raise, an all in and a call and the winner is down to the five cards dealt on the table. It is up to you to decide on the strength of your opponents play. You will, by now, have spent a considerable amount of time at the same poker table and should have developed an insight into the way they play. Assume that their range has also opened up and play accordingly.

Heads-up play is very specialized and unless you have practiced this way you will find that the final winner is often more down to fortune. Make sure that your starting cards are strong and apply pressure to the other player. If the other player re-raises you, you need to reassess the strength of your cards and act accordingly. Be aggressive and show no fear and you will be successful at least half of the time.

Final table deals

Often during final table play, especially when the number of players drops to two or three and the blinds rise high enough to make every chip stack small in comparison, players will suggest making a deal. As the blind levels increase the value of each chip decreases, just as it does I the early stages of the tournament. Once each player has a relatively low chip stack, around five BB each, then the skill level is reduced. The range of hands that players will commit with increases and more is left to chance than skill. For this reason players are often open to stopping the game and sharing the remaining prize money between the remaining players. This is a common situation. Heads-up play is so specialized that some players would rather deal than risk some prize money.

It is usually the chip leader that fists suggests a deal, after all, they are in the best position to win. In the situation where they are massively leading they will be unlikely to want o risk giving away some of the prize money as they will rightly think that they are in a good position to win.

If the chip stacks are more evenly distributed a deal is usually more likely to be offered.

The only real fair deal to accept is a deal that is based on the Independent Chip Model (ICM). This model calculates the effective value of each chip in play and divides the remaining prize money among players based on the chips they have in their stack. A pretty complicated way of doing things. They calculate the remaining prize money, count the total chips in play, assign a value for each chip and calculate each chip stacks worth.

Example

There are three players remaining in a tournament. The total remaining prize money is $560)$280 first, $165 second, $115 third)and there are 250000 chips in play in total. This means that each chip is worth 0.224 cents. (Simply divide the remaining prize money by the total number of chips)
If your chip stack is 89000 chips then your chip stack is worth $199.36 (the value of each chip multiplied by the number of chips you have in your stack.

Any deal suggested should offer you an approximate amount to this, the chip leader, by virtue of being the chip leader, often tried to broker a deal which gives him a slight prize money advantage, but you should decline any offer that does not mean that you get a fair payout. The offer of almost $200 is higher than either the second or third place payout so should be carefully considered. A deal always gives a better margin to players unlikely to win, but the chip leader also knows that they are not sure of winning so it might be a safe option.

The ICM model is an accurate model but can be complicated to work out at the table. The easiest method is proportional payout. Simply see what proportion of the total chips you have in front of you, in the example about, 89000 is just over a third of the total chips available. A third of the remaining prize money is almost $190. This gives a rough size of what your fair payout would be in a deal. Very rough calculations, but much easier to do quickly at a poker table.
If the deal offers you significantly less than your proportional share then you should decline the deal and play on till the end, even though only first place might offer you more winnings.

The general rule of thumb is that you should not accept much less than your proportional share, and should not ask for much more.
A fair deal in the example would give you prize money of around $180 - $190. Any other deal is unfair.

Remember that any deal must be agreed by all remaining players. A deal cannot be forced onto a player who for reasons of their own (money, confidence, enjoyment) wants to continue playing. It is also unfair to refuse a deal when you have a low chip stack and this a lower proportional share, only to suggest a deal when, after one successful hand, you now find yourself in a much better position. If a deal is refused the game is normally played to its full completion.

14

FINAL SUMMARY

If you have managed to read this book fully, without skipping sections. You are now prepared to take on the poker table armed with a good set of sound, proven, tools and ideas. Please don't think that you can win every hand, and some days you will lose more than you win. That is when your bankroll management becomes even more important. It is unreasonable to expect that every tournament you play will produce a cash win. Over time, however, tournament play should be profitable. By it's nature, you will lose more tournaments than you win but the profit margin in a good tournament win will prove to be profitable over a long term strategy.

You have an understanding of the strength of your hand pre flop, but you also have no idea of the strength of the hands of the other players. This is where watching each hand carefully, even if you have folded and are taking no further part, becomes important. Try to develop an understanding of how other players act and this will give indications, tells, of their hand strength.

You have an understanding of betting pre flop. General

guidelines have been give, if you wish to change and adapt these to suit your own style of play then feel free but remember to try and keep things consistent.

You have gained an understanding of the strength of made hands and of draw hands. But also try to appreciate that other players may also have made hands or draw hands. Moving forward into the area of estimating the strength of your opponents hand takes time and practice. Lots of practice, often non profitable practice. It is not unusual for developing players, indeed all players of all standards, to have losing games. The greatest and most profitable players of all times do not win every day they sit at the tables. Over time, they make a profit, they 'Grind' out the tables. Long slow profit.

Everyone hears of the one or two, well advertised, get rich quick poker tales of massive profits. Remember, if one person has made massive profits at a table it ALWAYS means that several other players have lost.

Making sure that you are not one of the losing players should always be your first priority. Winnings will come with time if you minimize the losing experiences. This is again down to your bankroll and your hand selection.

It is not uncommon for a tight-aggressive player to sit for long periods of time without actually playing a hand, folding all hole cards. On average you would expect, over an extended period of time, to be playing around 1 in nine or ten hands. 10%-15%. The rest of the hands are not strong enough or profitable enough to play.

Have patience, Poker is rarely a get rich quick game. Don't be frightened to fold if unsure. Trusting your money to the lap of the Gods of good fortune very rarely proves to be successful over the longer period of time.

Good luck at the tables, as you become more familiar with the guided approaches given in this book you will adapt them to suit your own style. Always try to keep a record of styles you use and how profitable you are. Be fluid in your approaches and never be afraid to pull things back to basics if you feel things are starting to go astray.

And finally, there is nothing stopping you from standing up from a table and leaving. Do not feel that you have to stay out of fair play if you have been successful. You do not need to give the other players a chance to win their money back. If you find that you are losing steadily on a table, leave. Cut your losses and move to another table, or give up for the day. It usually means that you are out of your depth, ability and skill wise, at that table. If you are losing, walk away. Never try to stay and win your money back. Pick an easier table, maybe at lower stakes with less experienced players.

Remember, avoiding losing is more important in the early days than winning enough to pay your mortgage.

15

POKER TERMINOLOGY

Bet – When a player commits chips to the pot it is called a bet

Call – When a player matches a previously made bet it is a call

Raise – When a player increases the bet after someone has already bet

Re raise – Also called a three-bet, when a player increases the bet for a third time, after the initial bet and the following raise

Fold – A player returns the hole cards to the dealer, and takes no further part in the hand

Check – A player declines to make a bet and passed the play to the next player, only if a bet has not already been placed

Pocket Pair – When both of your hole cards are of the same value.

Pre-flop – All action that takes place before the first

community cards are dealt is termed as being pre-flop

Post-flop – All action that takes place after the first three community cards are dealt is termed as post-flop

Draw – an as yet unmade hand which has the possibility of being completed with the remaining community cards. For example, four cards, all hearts, with just the first three community cards on show is a Flush Draw with two cards to come. Giving the possibility of one of the remaining two community cards being a heart and completing the flush

16

WHERE TO PLAY

Poker is literally a game that can be played anywhere because you need so little equipment to do so. Many people now organize home games playing against friends and family and many pubs also have small pub leagues.

If you have enough confidence in your game, you can also take on a casino game. These are the places where you will learn most. Reading a book and getting the game straight in your head is great, but it's through practice and facing different situations will the real learning take place.

Poker is a game that is constantly evolving, and it never gets boring, simply because you will face hundreds of different hands in hundreds of different positions against hundreds of different opponents, and each of these opponents will tackle the game with their own unique style. This is where your reading of people rather than the game comes into play!

Online poker is very popular now with many people making their living online.

Many sites now offer bonuses when you sign up, and it is definitely worth taking advantage of some of those as well as playing in their freeroll games where you will learn a lot.

Most of all enjoy it!

Lastly, if you have enjoyed this book you can get a free copy of my guide to online strategy by visiting this website.

http://poker.subscribemenow.com/